Presented to ....

From ....

Date ....

The Beautiful Promises of Allah

compiled by

RUQAIYYAH WARIS MAQSOOD

First published 1998

Reprinted 1999, 2001, 2003

Goodword Books Pvt. Ltd.
1, Nizamuddin West Market
New Delhi 110 013
Tel. 435 5454, 435 6666
Fax 435 7333, 435 7980
e-mail: info@goodwordbooks.com
website: www.goodwordbooks.com

INTRODUCTION

One of the most thought-provoking things that we human beings have learned about our Wonderful Creator, Allah, is that although our universe and everything it contains is in a constant state of flux and change, the Almighty One Who ordained it is utterly changeless and dependable.

We know that the only constant aspect of our immediate surroundings is that we cannot keep it the same; we cannot dip our toes into the same river twice. Those of us who have survived childhood, adolescence and adulthood and are now facing old age, or who have created gardens and parks, are all too aware of this.

Yet we know, of course that there are laws governing all the changes we perhaps wistfully observe. Farmers and gardeners are always conscious of the seasons, for example, and of the natural cycles of growth, maturity, fruition and 'death'.

Awareness of the laws on the grander scale of the universe has taken longer for humanity to grasp. Over the centuries, we have discovered many things. What we thought at first to be changes, or novelties, are now viewed in a much grander perspective; and we have gradually realised that the laws of the universe governing all the apparent changes and developments, are in fact immutable.

God does not change. Nor do His promises to us, whether we love Him, ignore Him, refuse to believe in Him, or spend all our lives in His service in a kind of superstitious 'finger-crossed' hopefulness.

The promises of Allah revealed in the Qur'an are not new. Most of them were revealed centuries before the revelations granted to the Messenger Muhammad, may peace be upon him.

Yet in the words that came to our Prophet, they were uttered afresh, touching hearts and lives in a new way, giving fresh hope and goals for our future state of the Hereafter.

This collection draws together most of the beautiful promises uttered in the Qur'an, full of blessing and grace, and boundless, compassionate love. For those who will receive it, it brings immense uprush of joy, and a feeling of overwhelming gratitude flooding through one's being.

May Allah be praised. Amen.

Ruqaiyyah Waris Maqsood
Hull (U.K.)

Have you taken a promise from God,
for He never breaks His promise?

(2:80)

This is the Book; (I promise you that) in it is sure guidance, with no doubts, for those who have reverence for God; who believe in the unseen, who are steadfast in prayer, who give to others out of what We have provided for them; and who believe in the revelation sent (both) to you (O Prophet) and that sent before your time; and who have firm confidence in the Hereafter. They are being guided by their Lord, and it is these who will prosper.

(2:1-5)

If, as is certain, My guidance comes to you, those follow it shall neither be afraid, nor shall they grieve.

(2:38)

O Children of Israel! Keep in your minds the favours which I bestowed upon you, and fulfil your covenant with Me as I (promised to) fulfil My covenant with you. Fear none but Me. Believe that which I (now) reveal, which confirms the revelation you have had already, and do not be the first to reject faith in it, nor sell My signs for a small price; fear Me, and Me alone. Do not cover truth with falsehood, nor conceal that which you know to be true. Be steadfast in prayer; practise regular charity; and bow down your heads with those who bow down. Are you demanding that the people should behave rightly, but you forget to practise right-living yourselves, even though you study the scriptures? Will you not understand? No, seek God's help with patient perseverance and prayer; it is indeed hard, except to those who bring a lowly spirit, who keep in mind the certainty that they are to meet their Lord, and that they are to return to Him.

(2:40-46)

Those who believe (in the Qur'an), and those who follow the Jewish (scriptures), and Christians and the Sabians - any who believe in God and the Last Day, and work righteousness, shall have their reward with their Lord; on them shall be no fear, neither shall they grieve.

(2:62; 5:72)

Those who believe and do good works, they are the Companions of the Garden; they will abide therein.

(2:82)

Allah will choose for His special mercy those whom He will; He is the Lord of Grace unbounding.

(2:105)

Be steadfast in prayer and give regularly in charity; and whatever good you send forth for your souls before you, you will find it with Allah; for God sees well everything that you do.

(2:110)

Whoever submits his (or her) whole self to Allah and is a doer of good - he (or she) will find their reward with the Lord; on such shall be no fear, neither shall they grieve.

(2:112)

The Jews say: 'The Christians have nothing (to stand) on', and the Christians say: 'The Jews have nothing (to stand) on'; yet they profess to study the (same) Book. The value of what is said by those who know nothing is about the same; Allah will judge between them in their disputes on the Day of Judgement.

(2:113)

To Allah belong the East and the West; whichever way you turn, you will find there the Presence of God. For God is All-Pervading, All-Knowing.

(2:115)

O Children of Israel! Call to mind the special favour which I bestowed upon you, and that I preferred you to all others (for My Message). Guard yourselves against a Day when (I promise you,) one soul shall not avail another, nor shall compensation be accepted from anyone, nor shall intercession profit anyone, nor shall anyone find (outside) help.

(2:122-123)

Those who reject faith - for a while I will allow them their pleasures, but soon I will drive them to the torment of Fire - an evil destination (indeed!).

(2:126)

They (i.e. people of the past, or any other folk) shall reap the fruit of what they did, and you of what you do!

(2:141)

God will never make your faith of no effect. For God is surely full of kindness, and most merciful to all people.

(2:143)

To every one of you is a goal towards which God turns you; so strive together towards all that is good. Wheresoever you are, God will bring you together; for God has power over all things.

(2:148)

Remember Me; I will remember you. Be grateful to Me, and do not reject faith.

(2:152)

Be sure that We shall test you with something of fear and hunger, some loss in goods, or lives, or the fruits of your toil; but give glad tidings to those who patiently persevere, who say when afflicted with calamity: 'To God we belong, and to Him is our return'. They are those on whom blessings from God and mercy (descend); they are the ones who are accepting their guidance.

(2:155-157)

Those who conceal the clear (Signs) We have sent down, and the guidance, after We have made it clear for the people in the Book - on them shall be God's curse, and the curse of those entitled to curse them - except for those who repent and make amends and openly declare (the Truth). To them I turn, for I am Oft-Returning, Most Merciful.

(2:159-160)

When My servants ask you concerning Me, I am indeed close (to them); I listen to the prayer of every suppliant when they call on Me; let them also, with a will, listen when I call, and believe in Me, that they may walk in the right way.

(2:186)

Fear Allah, and know that He is with those who restrain themselves.

(2:194)

Do good, for Allah loves those who do good.

(2:195)

The life of this world is alluring to those who reject faith, and who scoff at those who believe. But the righteous will be above them on the Day of Resurrection. God bestows His measureless abundance on whoever He chooses.

(2:212)

By His grace God guides believers to the truth concerning the matters that were dividing them; God guides whoever He wills to the path that is straight.

(2:213)

Truly, the help of Allah is always near!

(2:214)

Those who believed, and those who suffered exile, and those who fought in the path of God - they have the hope of the Mercy of Allah; Allah is Oft-Forgiving, Most Merciful.

(2:218)

Allah loves those whose regular practice is to turn to Him, and He loves those who keep themselves pure and clean.

(2:222)

Don't try to use 'doing God's (business)' as an excuse in your oaths against doing good, or acting in the right way, or making peace between people; for God hears and knows everything.

(2:224)

Allah will not call you to account for making thoughtless promises, but (He will consider) the intention in your hearts; He is Oft-Forgiving, Most Forbearing.

(2:225)

No soul shall have a burden laid on it greater than it can bear. No mother shall be treated unfairly on account of her child, nor father on account of his child. The offspring shall be chargeable in the same way.

(2:233)

Who will loan to God a beautiful loan, which will be doubled and multiplied many times? It is Allah Who gives you want or plenty, and to Him shall be your return.

(2:245)

Allah grants His authority to whom He pleases. God cares for all people and He knows everything.

Allah holds one set of people in check by means of another. If this was not His will, the earth would indeed be full of mischief; but His love is for all in boundless measure.

(2:251)

Let there be no forcing in matters of religion; Truth stands out clear from error. Whoever rejects evil and believes in God has grasped the most reliable handhold, one that will never break.

(2:256)

Allah is the Protector of those who have faith; He will lead them out of the depths of darkness into light.

(2:257)

Those who use that which they have been granted in the way of God are like a grain of corn that grows seven ears, each ear containing a hundred grains! God gives generous increase to those whom He pleases; He cares for everything and He knows everything.

(2:261)

Those who use that which they have been granted in the cause of God, and do not follow up their gifts with reminders of their generosity or with injury - their reward is with their Lord; on them shall be no fear, neither shall they grieve.

(2:262)

The Evil One threatens you with poverty, and tries to make you act in an unseemly manner. God promises you His forgiveness and His generous love. God cares for all, and knows everything.

(2:268)

Whatever you spend in charity or out of love, be sure God knows it all.

(2:270)

Whatever good you give shall be rendered back to you, and you shall not be dealt with unjustly.

(2:272)

Those who spend of their goods by night and by day, in secret and in public, have their reward with their Lord; on them shall be no fear, neither shall they grieve.

(2:274)

Those who believe and do deeds of righteousness, and establish regular prayers and charity, will have their reward with their Lord; on them shall be no fear, neither shall they grieve.

(2:277)

Do not deal unjustly, and you shall not be dealt with unjustly.

(2:279)

To God belongs everything that is in the heavens and on earth. Whether you show what is in your minds or conceal it, God will call you to account for it.

(2:284)

•

In God's sight are (all) His servants - those who say 'Our Lord, we have indeed believed; forgive us our sins, and save us from the agony of Fire.'

(3:15-16)

You cause the night to gain on the day, and cause the day to gain on the night; You bring the living out of the dead, and the dead out of the living; and You will sustain whosoever You please, without limits.

(3:27)

As to those who reject faith, they will be punished with terrible distress in this world and in the Hereafter, nor will they have anyone to help.

(3:56)

As to those who believe and work righteousness, God will pay them in full their due reward; but He does not love those who do wrong.

(3:57)

You will never attain righteousness unless you give freely of that which you love; and whatever you give, truly, God knows it well.

(3:92)

Whoever holds firmly to God will be shown a way that is straight.

(3:101)

If you remain firm and act aright, even if the enemy should rush on to you in hot haste, your Lord would help you with five thousand angels, making a terrific onslaught.

(3:125)

Do not lose heart, nor fall into despair; you will surely gain mastery if you are true in faith.

(3:139)

A soul cannot die, except by God's leave, the term having been fixed as by writing. If any do desire a reward in this life, We shall give it; and if any do desire a reward in the Hereafter, We shall give it. We shall reward swiftly those that (serve Us with) gratitude.

(3:145)

God is your Protector; He is the Best of Helpers.

(3:150)

And if you are slain, or die, in the way of God, forgiveness and mercy from Him are far better than all it is possible to amass. And if you die, or are slain, Lo! It is to God that you are brought together.

(3:157-158)

If God helps you, none can overcome you; if He forsakes you, who is there, after that, who could help you? In God, then, let believers put their trust.

(3:160)

Do not think of those who are slain in God's way as dead. No, they live, finding their sustenance in the Presence of their Lord.

(3:169)

Every soul shall have a taste of death; and only on the Day of Judgement shall you be paid your full recompense. Only the one who is saved far from the Fire and admitted to the Garden will have attained the object (of Life); for the life of this world is but goods and chattels of deception.

(3:185)

You shall certainly be tried and tested in your possessions and in your personal selves; and you shall certainly hear much that will grieve you from those who received the Book before you, and from those who worship many gods. If you persevere patiently, and guard against evil, that will be a determining factor in every affair.

(3:186)

I will never suffer the work of any of you to be lost, be you male or female; you are members one of another.

(3:195)

Those who have left their homes, or been driven out of them, or suffered harm in My cause, or fought or been slain - truly I will blot out from them their iniquities and admit them into gardens with rivers flowing beneath, a reward from the Presence of God; and from His presence is the best of rewards.

(3:195)

God ever watches over you.

(4:1)

God accepts the repentance of those who do evil in ignorance and then immediately repent; to them He will turn in mercy; for God is full of knowledge and wisdom.

(4:17)

The repentance (is of no avail) for those who persist in doing evil until death stares them in the face and (only then) they say: 'Now I truly repent;' nor of those who die still rejecting faith; for them We have prepared a punishment most grievous.

(4:18)

If you will but turn your backs on the most heinous of the things which you are forbidden to do, We shall expel out of you all the other evil in you, and admit you to a Gate of great honour.

(4:31)

God is never unjust in the least degree; if there is any good done, He doubles it, and gives from His own presence a great reward.

(4:40)

All who obey God and the Messenger are in the company of those on whom is the grace of God, of the prophets, the sincere, the witnesses, and the righteous. Ah! What a beauteous fellowship!

(4:69)

To the one who fights in the cause of God, whether slain or victorious - soon shall We give a reward of great value.

(4:74)

Whoever recommends and aids a good cause becomes a partner therein; and whoever recommends and aids an evil cause will share its burden.

(4:85)

Those who forsake their homes in the cause of God find many a refuge in the earth, wide and spacious. Should they die for God and His Messenger, as refugees from their homes, their reward is certain and owing to them from Allah.

(4:100)

People may hide (their crimes) from others, but they cannot hide them from Allah, seeing that He is in their midst - even when they plot during the darkness of night in words He cannot possibly approve; God will compass round all that they do.

(4:108)

If any person does evil or wrongs his (or her) own soul, but afterwards seeks God's forgiveness, that person will find God Oft-Forgiving, Most Merciful.

(4:110)

If any person is guilty of any fault or sin and throws it on to an innocent person, he (or she) will carry (the penalty) both for the flagrant sin and for the falsehood.

(4:112)

If it were not for the grace of God and His mercy towards you, some people would certainly have (succeeded in their) plots to lead you astray. But they will only lead their own souls astray, and will not be able to do the least harm to you. For God has sent down the Book and the Wisdom to you, and taught you that which you did not know. Boundless is the grace of God towards you.

(4:113)

Whoever forsakes God and takes Satan for a friend, of a surety that one has suffered a grievous loss.

(4:119)

Those who believe and do deeds of righteousness, We shall soon admit them to gardens with rivers flowing beneath, to dwell therein for ever. God's promise is truth; whose word can be truer than God's?

(4:122)

If any do deeds of righteousness - be they male or female – and have faith, they will enter heaven, and not the least injustice will be done to them.

(4:124)

If it were His will, O humanity, He could destroy you and create another race; for He has the power to do this.

(4:133)

We shall soon give their rewards to those who believe in God and His messengers, and make no distinction between any of them.

(4:152)

To those who believe and do deeds of righteousness, He will give the rewards they have earned, and much more, out of His bounty; but He will punish those who are arrogant and disdainful with a grievous penalty, nor will they find any, besides God, to protect or help them.

(4:173)

Those who believe in God, and hold fast to Him, He will soon admit to His mercy and grace, and guide them to Himself by a straight way.

(4:175)

In earlier times God took a promise from the Children of Israel, and appointed twelve captains among them. And God said: 'I am with you; if you but establish regular prayers, practise regular charity, believe in My messengers, honour and assist them, and loan to God a beautiful loan - truly I will wipe out from you your evils, and admit you to gardens with rivers flowing beneath; but if any of you, after this, resist faith, you will have truly wandered from the path of righteousness. But because of their breach of their promise We cursed them, and made their hearts grow hard; they changed the words from their (right) places, and forgot a good part of the message that was sent to them; nor will you cease to find them (except for a few) ever bent on new deceits. Yet, forgive them, and overlook (their misdeeds), for Allah loves those who are kind.

(5:13-14)

Also, from those who call themselves Christians, We did take a promise, but they forgot a good part of the message that was sent to them; so We have estranged them, with enmity and hatred between one sect of them and another, until the Day of Judgement. Soon God will reveal to them what it is they have done.

(5:15)

O people of the Book! Now there has come to you Our Messenger, revealing to you much that you used to conceal in the Book, and passing over much (that is now unnecessary). There has come to you a new light from God, and a clear Book, wherewith God guides all who seek His good pleasure to ways of peace and safety, and leads them by His will out of the darkness into the light, and guides them to a path that is straight.

(5:16-18)

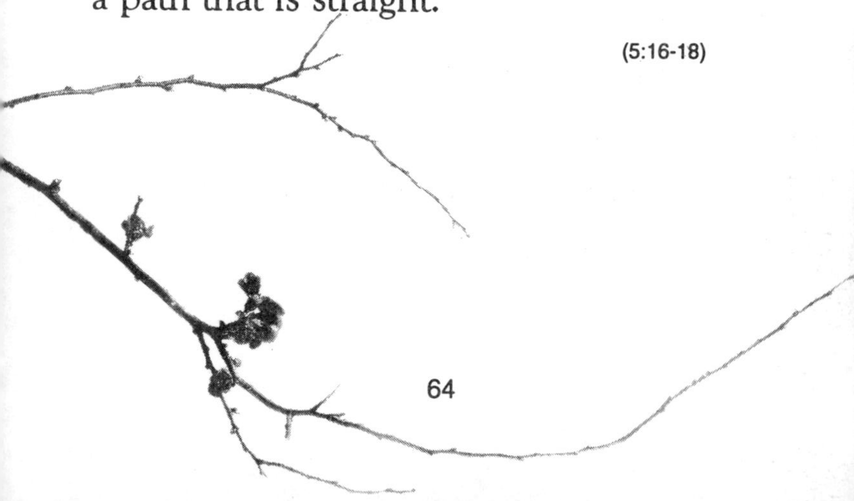

Jews and Christians both say: 'We are children of God, and His beloved ones.' Why then does He punish you for your sins? No, you are only people, of the many people He has created. He forgives whom He pleases, and He punishes whom He pleases. To God belongs the dominion of the heavens and the earth and all that is between, and to Him is the final goal (of all).

(5:20)

We ordained for you (the limit of revenge): 'Life for life, eye for eye, nose for nose, ear for ear, tooth for tooth, and wounds equal for equal.' But if any person forgoes that retaliation as an act of charity, it will be (counted as) an act of atonement for his (or her) own self.
And if any fails to judge by what God has revealed, they will have committed sin.

(5:48)

God will not hold you to account for meaningless oaths (uttered without thought), but He will call you to account for deliberate oaths. To put this right, you should feed ten poor people with the same sort of food as you would give to your own family; or clothe them; or give freedom to a slave. If that is beyond your means, then fast for three days. That will be acceptable expiation for the oaths you have sworn. But you should keep your promises. Thus does God make His signs clear to you, that you may feel gratitude.

(5:89)

O believers! Guard your own souls. If you follow right guidance, those who stray will not be able to hurt you. The goal of you all is to God; it is He Who will show you the truth of all that you do.

(5:108)

If God touches you with affliction, none can remove it but He; if He touches you with happiness – He has power over all things.

(6:17)

What is the life of this world but play and amusement? Best is the home in the Hereafter, for those who are righteous.

(6:32)

Only those who listen can respond to the call; as to the dead, God (alone) can raise them up; then will they be turned unto Him.

(6:36)

Do not send away those who call on their Lord morning and evening, seeking His face. You are not accountable in any matter pertaining to them, and they are not accountable for you, that you should turn them away, and thus be among those that do evil.

(6:52)

With Him are the keys of the Unseen, the treasures none knows but He. He knows all that there is on and in the sea. Not a leaf falls but with His knowledge. There is not a grain in the darkness of the earth, nor anything green or withered, but it is in a clear Record.

(6:59)

It is He Who takes your souls by night, and has knowledge of all that you do by day; by day He raises you up again, that the term appointed be fulfilled. In the end, to Him will be your return, and He will show you the truth of all that you did.

(6:60)

He is the Irresistible, watching over His worshippers. And He sets guardians over you. At length, when death approaches any of you, Our angels take his (or her) soul, and they will never fail in their duty.

(6:61)

This is the guidance of God; He gives that guidance as He wills to those of His worshippers He chooses. If they were to worship other things or persons as deities besides Him, then all that they did for them would be quite futile.

(6:88)

Behold! You will come to Us naked and alone, as We created you in the first place. You will leave behind you all the (favours) which We bestowed upon you. We will not see with you those who interceded for you, whom you considered to be partners in your affairs. All bonds between you (and your earthly life) will have been cut off, and your confidence in vain beliefs will have forsaken you.

(6:94)

Your Lord knows best who strays from His way; He knows best who receives His guidance.

(6:117)

God knows best how to carry out His mission. Soon the wicked will be overtaken by humiliation before God, and a severe punishment for all their evil scheming.

(6:124)

This is the Way of your Lord, leading straight; We have detailed the signs for those prepared to receive guidance. For them there will be a Home of Peace in the Presence of their Lord; He will be their Friend, because they practised righteousness.

(6:126-127)

Your Lord would not destroy people's habitations for their wrongdoings without giving them warning.

(6:131)

All that has been promised to you will come to pass; you cannot prevent the very least part of it.

(6:134)

Those who ignorantly and foolishly slay their children, and forbid them the food which God has provided for them, inventing lies against God, are lost; they have indeed gone astray and not listened to guidance.

(6:140)

This is a Book which We have revealed as a blessing; if you follow it and are righteous, you will receive mercy.

(6:155)

As for those who are divisive in their religion, and break up into sects, do not have the least part to do with in them. The matter lies before God; He will in the end enlighten them as to what they did.

(6:159)

The one that does good shall receive ten times as much to his (or her) credit; but the one that does evil shall only be paid back according to the extent of their evil; no injustice shall be done to them.

(6:160)

We shall remove from their hearts any lurking sense of injury; beneath them will be flowing rivers, and they shall say: 'Blessed be God, Who has guided us to this great happiness; we could never have found the way, had it not been for the guidance of God. It really was the truth that the messengers of our Lord brought to us.' As they will hear the cry: 'Behold! The Garden lies before you! You have been made its inheritors, for your deeds of righteousness.'

(7:43)

O believers! If you have reverence for God, He will grant you a Criterion (to judge between right and wrong), remove all evil afflicting you, and forgive you; for He is the Lord of grace unbounded.

(8:29)

Obey God and His Messenger; do not fall into disputes, lest you lose heart and power departs. Be patient and persevering, for God is with those who patiently persevere.

(8:46)

Whatever you spend in the cause of God shall be repaid unto you, and you will not be treated unjustly.

(8:60)

Those who believe, and suffer exile, and strive with might and main in God's cause with their goods and their persons, have the highest rank in the sight of God; they are the people who will achieve salvation.

(9:20)

The promise of God is sure and true. It is He Who begins the process of creation, and repeats it, that He may reward justly those who believe and work righteousness; but those who reject Him will (as it were) have to drink boiling fluids, a grievous penalty, because they rejected Him.

(10:4)

Those who have earned evil will have a reward of like evil; their faces will be covered with ignominy; there will be none to defend them from the wrath of God; their faces will be covered, as it were, with pieces from the depths of the darkness of night; they are companions of the Fire; they will abide therein for ever.

(10:27)

There, every soul will prove the deeds it sent on ahead; they will be brought back to God, their rightful Lord, and any invented falsehoods will leave them in the lurch.

(10:30)

Truly, God will not deal unjustly with humanity in anything; it is people who wrong their own souls.

(10:44)

One day He will gather them together; it will be as if they had waited no more than one hour of a day. They will recognise each other. However, those who denied the meeting with God and refused to receive true guidance will be lost.

(10:45)

God will not allow the work of those who make mischief to prosper.

(10:81)

For those who show patience and constancy, and work righteousness - for them is forgiveness and a great reward.

(11:11)

Those who desire the life and glitter of the present world - to them We shall pay the price of their deeds in it, without any diminution. There is nothing for them in the Hereafter but the Fire.

(11:15-16)

Those who try to hinder people from the path of God, and would seek in it something crooked - these are they who deny the Hereafter. They will in no wise frustrate (His design) on earth, nor will they have any protectors besides God! They will earn double penalty. They have lost the power to hear, and they did not see!

(11:19-20)

But those who believe and work righteousness, and are humble before their Lord – they will be companions of the Garden, to dwell therein for ever.

(11:23)

When the Appointed Day arrives, no soul shall speak except by His leave; of those gathered some will be wretched and some will be blessed. Those who are wretched shall be in the Fire; there will be for them sighing and weeping. They will remain there for as long as the heavens and the earth endure, except as the Lord wills – for your Lord is the (certain) Accomplisher of that which He planned. And those who are blessed shall be in the Garden; they will remain there for all the time that the heavens and earth endure, except as your Lord wills; an uninterrupted gift.

(11:105-108)

Be certain that your Lord will pay back to all (the full recompense) of their deeds; He knows all that they do.

(11:111)

Be steadfast in patience; for truly God will not suffer the reward of the righteous to perish.

(11:115)

For each (person) there are (angels) in succession, before and behind; they guard each one by God's command. Truly, God will never change the condition of a people until they change it themselves (within their own souls). When God wills a people's punishment to come, there can be no turning it back, nor will they find, besides Him, any to protect.

(13:11)

Those who patiently persevere, seeking the countenance of their Lord; establish regular prayers; spend, out of the gifts We have bestowed for their sustenance, both in secret and openly; and turn away evil with good - for such there is the final attainment of the Eternal Home, the gardens of eternal bliss. They shall enter there, as well as those of their parents, spouses and offspring who are righteous; and angels shall go in to them from every gate (with the salutation): 'Peace be unto you because of your patient perseverance. Now, how excellent is your final Home.'

(13:22-24)

Truly, God leaves to stray whom He will; but He guides to Himself those who turn to Him in penitence, those who believe and whose hearts find satisfaction in the remembrance of God; for without doubt, hearts do find satisfaction in the remembrance of God. For those who believe and do righteous deeds is blessedness, a beautiful place of return.

(13:28-29)

God will make firm in strength those who believe, with the Word that stands firm, in this world and in the Hereafter; but God will leave to stray those who do wrong.

(14:27)

One day the earth will be changed to a different earth, and so will the Heavens. And people will be marshalled forth, before God, the One, the Irresistible. And you will see the wicked on that day tied together with chains, their garments of liquid pitch, and their faces covered with Fire. God will requite each soul according to its just deserts; and truly God is swift in calling to account. This is a message for humanity; let them take warning from it, and let them realise that He is the One God; let those who understand take heed!

(14:48-52)

We never destroyed a population that had not a term decreed and assigned beforehand. A people can neither anticipate the Term, nor delay it.

(15:4-5)

The righteous (will be) amid gardens and fountains: 'Enter ye here in peace and security!' And We shall remove from their hearts any lurking sense of injury; (they will be) brothers, facing each other on thrones. No sense of fatigue shall touch them, nor shall they (ever) be asked to leave.

(15:45-48)

If you tried to count up the favours of Allah, you would never be able to number them; God is the Oft-Forgiving, the Most Merciful.

(16:18)

They swear by their strongest oaths that God will not raise to life again those that die. No, surely it is a truthful promise, but most of humanity does not realise it.

(16:38)

To those who leave their homes in Allah's cause, who have suffered oppression, we will assuredly give them a goodly home in this world; but the greater reward will be that of the Hereafter.

(16:41)

If Allah were to punish people for their wrong-doings, no single living being would be left on earth; but He gives them a chance, for a stated term; (however), when that term runs out, they will not be able to delay (the punishment) for a single hour, just as they may not bring it forward by a single hour.

(16:61)

What is with you must vanish away; what is with God will last for ever. And We will certainly bestow their reward according to the best of their actions on those who patiently persevere.

(16:96)

Whoever works righteousness, man or woman, and has faith, truly to that person We will give a new life, a life that is good and pure; and We will bestow on such their reward, according to the best of their actions.

(16:97)

One day, every soul will come up struggling for itself, and every soul will be fully recompensed for all its actions, and none shall be unjustly dealt with.

(16:111)

We have fastened every person's fate on his (or her) own neck. On the Day of Judgement We will bring out for each person a scroll, which he (or she) will see spread open. It will be said: 'Read your own record; your own soul is sufficient this day to make out your own account.

(17:13-14)

Whoever receives guidance receives it for his (or her) own benefit; whoever goes astray does so to his (or her) own loss. No bearer of burdens will bear the burden of anyone else; nor would We visit Our anger on anyone without sending a Messenger first (to give warning).

(17:15)

Do not abort your children because you fear you will not be able to support them through your circumstances; We will sustain them, as well as you. Truly, if you kill them, that is a great sin.

(17:31)

One day, We shall call together all human beings with their respective imams; those who are given their record in their right hand will read it (with pleasure), and they will not be dealt with unjustly in any least way. But those who were blind in this world, will be blind in the Hereafter, and far astray from the Path.

(17:71-72)

As to those who believe and do good works, truly We will not suffer to perish the reward of any who do any righteous deed. There will be Gardens of Eternity for them, with flowing rivers beneath; they will be adorned with golden bracelets, and wear garments of fine green silk and heavy brocade; they will take their ease on raised thrones. How good that reward - what a beautiful couch to take ease on!

(18:30-31)

One Day, We shall remove the mountains, and you will see the earth as a level plain; and We shall gather all together, and shall not leave out a single person.

(18:47)

We shall save those who guarded themselves against evil, and We shall leave the wrongdoers (humbled) to their knees.

(19:72)

We created you from the earth, and We shall return you into it; and from it We will bring you out once again.

(20:55)

Every soul shall have a taste of death; and We test you by evil and by good, as trials. To Us you must return.

(21:35)

We will set up scales of justice for the Day of Judgement, so that not one soul will be dealt with unjustly in the least. And if there be no more than the weight of a mustard-seed, We will bring it into account.

(21:47)

We listened to him (Dhun-nun), and delivered him from his distress. Thus do We deliver all those who have faith.

(21:88)

Whoever works any act of righteousness and has faith, his (or her) endeavour will not be rejected: We shall record it in his (or her) favour.

(21:94)

When the True Promise draw nigh, then behold! The eyes of the unbelievers will be in a fixed stare of horror. (They will cry): 'Ah! Woe to us! We refused to take heed of this; we truly did wrong!

(21:97)

Those for whom the good record from Us has already been recorded, will be removed far from Hell; they will not hear the slightest sound of it. Whatever their souls desired, in that will they dwell. The Great Terror will bring them no grief, but the angels will meet them, (saying): 'This is your day, the day you were promised.'

(21:101-103)

The Day that We roll up the heavens like a scroll, even as We produced the first creation, so shall We produce the new one; a promise We have undertaken—truly We shall fulfil it.

(21:104)

Truly, the Hour will come; there can be no doubt about it, or about (the fact) that God will raise to life all who are at that time in the grave.

(22:7)

Truly, God will defend those who believe; truly He does not love those who are traitors to faith, or those who show ingratitude.

(22:38)

God will certainly aid those who aid His cause–truly, He is Full of Strength, Exalted in Might, and able to see His will come to pass.

(22:40)

Those who leave their homes in God's cause, and are then killed or die (of other causes), on them God will surely bestow a goodly Provision; truly God is He Who bestows the best Provision. Truly, He will admit them to a place with which they shall be well pleased.

(22:58-59)

If a person has retaliated to no greater extent than the injury received, and is once again set upon, God will come to his (or her) aid. For God is One Who blots out and forgives.

(22:60)

It is He Who gave you life, and will cause you to die, and will give you life again.

(22:66)

God will judge between you on the Day of Judgement concerning any matter over which you differed.

(22:69)

On the Day of Judgement you will be raised up again.

(23:16)

When the Trumpet is blown, the physical relationship that had existed between people on earth will not exist that day, nor will one ask after another.

(23:101)

Those who slander chaste women who are believers but who have acted indiscreetly–they are cursed in this life and in the Hereafter; a grievous punishment awaits them.

(24:23)

The state of unbelievers will be like the depths of darkness in a vast deep ocean, overwhelmed by billow upon billow, with dense clouds looming overhead; depths of darkness, one above another. If a person stretched out a hand, he (or she) would hardly see it. To any person to whom God does not give light, there is no light!

(24:40)

If a person repents and believes and does righteous deeds, God will change the evil of such persons into good; God is Oft-Forgiving, Most Merciful.

(25:70)

Whoever repents and does good has truly turned to God with an (acceptable) conversion.

(25:71)

Those who pray: 'Our Lord! Grant us spouses and offspring who will be the comfort of our eyes, and give us the grace to lead the righteous'—those are the ones who will be rewarded with the highest place in heaven, for their patient constancy.

(25:74-75)

If any have done wrong, but have thereafter substituted good in the place of evil, truly I am Oft-Forgiving, Most Merciful.

(27:11)

Truly, your Lord knows all that is hidden in their hearts, as well as all that they do openly. There is nothing of the Unseen, in heaven or earth, but it is recorded in a clear record.

(27:74-75)

You see the mountains, and think them firmly fixed (for ever); but they shall pass away as the clouds pass away.

(27:88)

It is true that you will not be able to guide every one whom you love; but God guides whom He will. And He knows best those who receive guidance.

(28:56)

Any who have repented, believed, and done righteous deeds, will have hopes to be among those who achieve salvation.

(28:67)

The Home of the Hereafter shall be given to those who did not intend to act high handedly or cause mischief on the earth.

(28:83)

If any do good, their reward will be better than that deed; but if any do evil, they will only be punished to the actual extent of the deeds they did (and not more than that)

(28:84)

Do not call on any other deity besides God. There is no God but He. Everything will perish, except His Own Face. To Him belongs the Command, and to Him will you all be brought back.

(28:88)

Those who believe and live doing righteous deeds, from them shall We blot out all evil in them, and We shall reward them according to the best of their deeds.

(29:7)

We have requested people to be kind to their parents; but if those parents try to make you worship partners with Me, any (so-called spirit forces) which are pure speculation, do not obey them. You have to return to Me, and then I will prove to you that you acted rightly.

(29:8; see also 31:15)

God knows with absolute certainty those who believe, and just as certainly He knows who the hypocrites are.

(29:11)

You will not be able to put blocks in the way of God's Plan either on earth or in heaven; nor do you have, besides God, any who can protect or help you.

(29:22)

Recite what is sent of the Book to you by inspiration, and establish regular prayer; for your prayer will hold you back from committing unjust and shameful deeds. Remembrance of God is without doubt the most important (thing in life). And (be sure) God knows everything that you do.

(29:45)

Can people not see that We have created a secure sanctuary for those (who believe), while all around them people are being snatched away (by fear and despair)? Why should they then cling to belief in that which is useless, and reject the grace of God? Who has done more harm than the person who invents falsehoods about (the nature of) God, or who rejects the truth even when it is presented (clearly) before him? Will the (proper) home not be in Hell for those who deny the truth? But for those who strive hard on Our behalf—We will certainly guide them to Our paths; truly God is with those who act rightly.

(29:67-69)

With God is the Decision; in the past and in the future. The believers will rejoice on that Day, with God's help. He helps whom He will, and he is Exalted in Might, Most Merciful. (This is) the promise of God. God never deviates from His promises; but most of humanity does not understand. They only know the outer (things) of the life of this world, and pay no heed to (what is to come,) the End of all things.

(30:4-7)

In the long run, evil in the extreme will be the end of those who do evil, in that they rejected (all) the Signs of God, and held them up to ridicule.

(30:10)

On the Day that the Hour will be established, the guilty will be struck dumb with despair. None of the things they thought of as powerful entities will be able to intercede for them, and they will themselves reject those so-called 'partners-of-God' (at last).

(30:12-13)

On the Day that the Hour will be established, all people will be sorted out. Those who have believed and done righteous deeds will find happiness in a Garden of Delight, and those who rejected faith and falsely denied Our Signs and the fact that there would be a meeting in the Hereafter, shall be brought forth to punishment.

(30:14-16)

So give glory to God when the evening falls, and when you rise in the morning; yea, praise Him, in the heavens and on earth, and when the shadows lengthen and the day begins to decline. It is He Who brings out the living from the dead, and the dead from the living, and Who gives life to the earth after it is dead; and in like manner shall you be brought out (from the dead).

(30:17-19)

Those who reject faith will suffer from that rejection.

(30:44)

Persevere with patience; for assuredly the promise of God is true. Do not let those who have no certainty of faith be able to shake your firmness.

(30:60)

Whoever submits his (or her) whole self to God, and actively does good deeds, that person has truly grasped the most trustworthy handhold; and with God rests the End and Decision of all affairs.

(31:22)

O humanity! Do your duty to your Lord, and have respect for (the coming of) the Day when no father can avail anything for his own son, nor a son for his father. Truly, the promise of God is certain: so do not let this present life deceive you, nor let the Chief Deceiver lead you astray about God.

(31:33)

No person knows what delights of the eye are kept concealed for them - as the reward for their good deeds.

(32:17)

Running away will not help you if you are running away from death or slaughter; and even if (you do escape), you will not be able to enjoy more than a brief respite. Who can screen you from God if it is His wish to give you either punishment or mercy? You will not find protector or helper for yourselves besides God.

(33:16-17)

Men and women who have surrendered,
believing men and believing women,
obedient men and obedient women,
truthful men and truthful women,
men and women who are patient and steadfast,
humble men and humble women,
men and women who give in charity,
men who fast and women who fast,

men and women who guard their chastity,
men and women who are ever mindful of God–
on them God will bestow forgiveness
and a rich reward.

(33:35)

It is not your wealth nor your descendants that will bring you nearer to Us in degree; but only those who believe and work righteousness - those are the ones for whom there is a multiplied reward for their deeds, while they dwell secure in the dwellings on high.

(34:37)

What God bestows out of His mercy upon humanity, there is none can withhold; and what He withholds, no-one can grant it.

(35:2)

If God were to punish people according to what they deserve, there would not be left on the earth a single living creature; but He gives them respite for a stated term. When that term expires, then be sure that God has in His sight all His servants (and none will escape His vigilance).

(35:45)

Truly, We shall give life to the dead; and We record all that they sent on before them, and the effects on what they left behind; We have taken account of everything in a clear Book of evidence.

(36:12)

On that Day not one soul will be wronged over the least detail; you shall simply be repaid that which was earned by your past deeds.

(36:54)

O servants of God who have transgressed against your own souls! Do not despair of the mercy of God; for God forgives every sin - He is Oft-Forgiving, Most Merciful.

(39:53)

Turn to your Lord, and bow to His will, before the penalty comes on you. After that moment, you shall not be helped.

(39:54)

God will deliver the righteous to their place of salvation. No evil will touch them, and they will not grieve.

(39:61)

You will see the angels surrounding the Throne on all sides, singing glory and praise to their Lord. The decision between them will be in justice, and the cry will be: 'Praise be to Allah, the Lord of the Worlds.

(39:75)

O My people! This life of the present world is nothing but for your use (for a time); it is the Hereafter that is the lasting Home.

(40:39)

The one who does evil will only be paid back for it to the degree of what was done; but the one who did good and is a believer–whether man or woman–such will enter the Garden and have an immeasurable reward.

(40:40)

The Hour will certainly come; let there be no doubt about it! Yet most people do not believe it.

(40:59)

Call on Me, and I will answer your prayer.

(40:60)

It is certain that those who are too arrogant to serve Me will (one day) find themselves in Hell–in humiliation.

(40:60)

It is He Who gives life and death; and when He decides upon any matter, He (only) says 'Be!', and it is.

(40:68)

Persevere in patience; for the promise of God is certain. And whether We show you (in this life) some part of what We promised, or We take your soul (to Our mercy before that), (in either case) it is to Us that you shall return.

(40:77)

It is certain that We will give the unbelievers a taste of a severe penalty, and We requite them for the worst of their deeds.

(41:27)

Soon We will show them Our signs in the (furthest) regions (of the earth) and in their own souls, until it becomes crystal clear to them that this is the truth.

(41:53)

(The Gardens of Bliss) is (the Bounty) of which God gives glad tidings to His servants who believe and do good deeds. Say: 'No reward do I ask of you for this, except the love of those near of kin.' And if anyone earns any good, We shall give that person an increase of good in respect of it; for God is Oft-Forgiving, Most Ready to Appreciate.

(42:23)

Whatever misfortune happens to you is because of the things your own hands have wrought; and for many of these He grants forgiveness.

(42:30)

Whatever you receive on earth is but (temporary), and for the convenience of this life; but that which is with God is better and more lasting. (It is) for those who believe and put their trust in their Lord; those who avoid the greater crimes and shameful deeds; those who, even when they are angry, forgive; those who listen to their Lord, and establish regular prayers; who conduct their affairs by mutual consultation; who spend out of what We bestow on them for sustenance; and those who, when an oppressive wrong is inflicted on them, help and defend themselves. The recompense of an injury is an injury equal to it (in degree); but if a person forgives and accepts reconciliation, he (or she) will be rewarded by God; for God does not love those who do wrong. However, if any do help and defend themselves after a wrong done to them, against such there is no cause of blame. The blame is only on those who oppress people with (various) wrongdoings, and insolently transgress beyond acceptable limits throughout the land, defying right and justice; for such there will be a grievous penalty. But if any show patience and forgive, that would truly be the exercise of a courageous will, and showing resoluteness in the conduct of affairs.

(42:36-43)

If any person withdraws from remembrance of the Most Gracious, We will appoint for that person an evil one, to be his (or her) intimate companion. Such (evil ones) really hinder them from the Path, even though they think they are being rightly guided.

(43:36-37)

(Jesus) will be the sign (for the coming of) the Hour (of Judgement); therefore have no doubt about the Hour, but follow Me; this is the Straight Way.

(43:61)

Tell those who believe to forgive those who do not look forward to the Days of God; (it is not for them to add to the punishment of unbelievers;) it is for Him to recompense all people according to what they have earned. If anyone performs one righteous deed, it will last for ever to the benefit of his (or her) own soul; if one does something evil, it works against (his or her own soul.

(45:14-15)

God created the heavens and the earth for just ends, and in order that each soul may find the recompense of what it has earned; and none of them will be treated unjustly.

(45:22)

Those who believe and work deeds of righteousness, and believe in the (Revelation) sent down to Muhammad–for it is the Truth from their Lord–He will remove from them their ills and improve their condition.

(47:2)

He (lets you fight) in order to test you, some with others. But those who are slain in the way of God–He will never let their deeds be lost. Soon will He guide them, and improve their condition, and admit them to the Garden which He has promised for them.

(47:4-6)

O you who believe! If you will aid (the cause of) God, He will aid you, and plant your feet firmly.

(47:7)

Do not be weary and faint-hearted, begging to find peace, when you should be uppermost. For God is with you, and will never put in loss for your (good) deeds.

(47:35)

It was We Who created humanity, and We know what dark suggestions their souls make to them; for We are nearer to them than their jugular vein. Behold, two (guardian angels) have been appointed to learn and note (their doings), one sitting on the right and one on the left; not a word does a person utter, but there is a watcher close by to record it. The stupor of death will bring the truth (before their eyes): 'This was the thing which you were trying to escape!' And the trumpet shall be blown; that will be the Day of which warning had been given. And every soul will come forth; and with each will be an angel to drive and an angel to bear witness. (It will be said): 'You took no heed of this; now We have removed your veil, and you will have sharp eyes this day! And your companion-angels will say: 'Here is (the record) ready with me!

(50:16-23)

Those who believe and whose families follow them in faith–We shall reunite them with their families; nor shall We deprive them (of the fruit) of any of their works; even so, each individual is in pledge for his (or her) own deeds.

(52:21)

No matter how many be the angels in the heavens, their intercessions will avail nothing except after God has given leave for those whom He pleases; and that person is acceptable to Him.

(53:26)

Shun those who turn away from Our message and desire nothing but the life of this world. That is as far as knowledge will reach them. Truly your Lord knows well those who stray from His path, and he knows those who receive guidance.

(53:29-30)

Those who avoid the great sins and shameful deeds, only (falling into) small faults–truly your Lord is ample in forgiveness. He knows you well when He brings you out of the earth, and when you are in your mother's wombs. Therefore, you have no need to justify yourselves; He knows already who it is that guards against evil.

(53:32)

Soon the multitude (of your enemies) will be put to flight, and they will show their backs.

(54:45)

Everything they do is recorded in their Book (of deeds). Every matter, no matter how small or great, is on record.

(54:32-33)

No frivolity will they hear (in the Garden of Bliss), nor any taint of evil - only the saying: 'Peace! Peace.

(56:25-26)

We have created for the companions of the right hand (partners who are) a special creation, and made them completely without stain of sin, beloved, and equal in age.

(56:35-38)

We have decreed Death to be the experience of all of you, and nothing will prevent Us from changing your forms and creating you (afresh) in (forms) that you cannot yet know.

(56:60-61)

One Day, you will see the believing men and women—how their light runs forward before them, and by their right hands; they will be greeted: 'What good news for you this Day! Gardens beneath which rivers flow! To be able to live there for ever! This is indeed the highest achievement.

(57:12)

No misfortune can happen on earth or in your souls but is recorded in a decree before We bring it into existence; truly, this is easy for God; (it is) in order that you may not despair over matters that pass you by, nor exult over favours bestowed upon you. For God does not love any vainglorious boaster.

(57:22-23)

Secret counsels are (inspired) by none but the Evil One, in order that he may cause upset to the believers; but he cannot harm them in the least, except as God allows; in God let the believers put their trust.

(58:10)

It may be that God will grant love between you and those whom you now hold as enemies. For God has power, and is Oft-Forgiving, Most Merciful.

(60:7)

O believers! Do not depend on people who have incurred the wrath of God. They have already lost their hope of the Hereafter, just as those who do not believe are in despair concerning those who are in their graves.

(60:13)

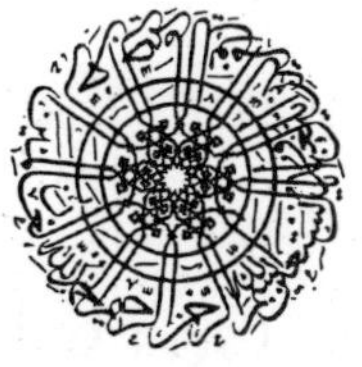

O believers! Why do you preach that which you do not practise? It is grievously odious in the sight of God that you say that which you do not do.

(61:2-3)

Truly, God loves those who fight in His cause in battle array, as if they were a solid concrete wall.

(61:4)

Those who invent falsehoods (against God) wish to extinguish God's Light with their mouths; but God will complete His Light, even though the unbelievers may detest it.

(61:8)

He will forgive you your sins, and admit you to Gardens beneath which rivers flow, and to beautiful mansions in Gardens of Eternity; that is indeed the supreme achievement.

(61:12)

And another (favour He will bestow), which you will love; help from God and a speedy victory. So give this good news to the believers.

(61:13)

The parable of those who were charged with the (obligations of the) Law of Moses, but who subsequently failed in them, is that of a donkey carrying weighty books (without understanding them). Calamitous is the parable of those who are bent on giving the lie to God's message; God does not bestow His guidance on such evildoing people.

(62:5)

The death from which you flee will nevertheless overtake you; then will you be sent back to the Knower of the things secret and open; and He will let you understand (the truth) of the things that you did.

(62:8)

O believers! Do not let your wealth or your children divert you from the remembrance of God. If any act like that, the loss is their own.

(63:9)

God will not grant respite to any soul when the time appointed for it has come; and God is well acquainted with all that you do.

(63:11)

No kind of calamity can occur, except by God's leave; if any person (truly) believes in God, God will guide his (or her) heart; for God knows all things.

(64:11)

O believers! Truly, among your spouses and your children are (some that are) enemies to yourselves; so beware of them. But if you forgive, and overlook, and cover up their faults, truly God is Oft-Forgiving, Most Merciful.

(64:14)

If you loan to God a beautiful loan, He will double it to your credit, and He will grant you forgiveness; for God is most ready to appreciate, Most Forbearing.

(64:17)

For those who fear God, He always prepares a way out.

(65:2)

And He provides for (those that reverence Him) from (sources) that person could never imagine. And if any one puts their trust in God, God will be sufficient for them.

(65:3)

If anyone reverences God, He will remove their ills and enlarge their reward.

(65:5)

God will never burden any person beyond what He has given that one. After every difficulty, God will be swift to grant relief.

(65:7)

If you turn in repentance to Him, (it means) your hearts are indeed turned in this way; but if you connive with each other against somebody, truly God is his (or her) Protector, and Gabriel, and every righteous one among those who believe–and furthermore, the angels will back him (or her) up.

(66:4)

As for those who fear their Unseen Lord, for them is forgiveness and a great reward. And whether you conceal your word or make it public, He certainly has full knowledge of the secrets of all hearts.

(67:12-13)

It is He Who has multiplied you through the earth, and to Him shall you be gathered together. They ask: 'When will this promise be fulfilled–if you are speaking the truth?' Say: 'As to knowledge of the time, it is with God alone. I am only sent to warn plainly in public.' In the end, when they see it close at hand, the faces of the unbelievers will be in grief, and it will be said (to them): 'This is that which you were calling for, (the promise fulfilled).

(67:24-27)

Do not pay attention to the type of despicable person, ready with oaths, a slanderer, going about with unpleasant stories, hindering good, transgressing beyond bounds, deep in sin, violent and cruel, base-born - because he possesses wealth and (numerous) sons. When Our Signs are told before him, he sneers: 'Old fables!' Soon We shall brand this beast on the snout!

(68:10-16)

Those who respect their trusts and promises, and those who are reliable in their witness;
and those who guard the (sacredness) of their worship—such will be honoured ones in the Gardens of Bliss.

(70:32-35)

God has produced you from the earth, growing, and in the end He will return you into it, and raise you forth (again at the Resurrection).

(71:17-18)

One day the earth and the mountains will be in violent commotion, and the mountains will be no more than a heap of sand poured out and flowing down.

(73:14)

Your Lord knows that you stand forth (in prayer) nearly two-thirds of the night, or half the night, or a third of the night, and so do some of those who are with you. And God, who determines the measure of night and day is aware that you would never keep count of it. So, He turns towards you (in His mercy); recite, therefore, as much of the Qur'an as may be easy for you. He knows that there may be some among you who have poor health; others are travelling through the land, seeking God's bounty; yet others are fighting for the cause. Therefore, recite (only) as much of the Qur'an as you may do with ease; and be constant in prayer and give regular charity, and loan to God a beautiful loan.

(73:20)

God leaves to stray whom He pleases, and guides whom He pleases; and none can understand the forces of your Lord, save Him alone. And this is a warning to humanity.

(74:31)

Every soul will be held in pledge for its deeds.

(74:38)

Does humanity think that We cannot re-assemble his bones? Nay, We are able to put together in perfect order even his fingerprints.

(75:3-4)

For the righteous, there will be a fulfilment of the heart's desires; enclosed gardens and vines, companions of equal age, and a cup full (to the brim).

(78:31-34)

The Day that they see it, (it will be) as if they had waited but a single evening, or no more than the next morning.

(79:46)

Truly, angels are appointed over you to protect you - kind and honourable, writing down your deeds. They know all that you do.

(82:10-12)

Woe to those who deal in fraud; those who, when they have to receive by measure from others exact full measure, but when they have to give by measure or weight to others, give less than their due. Do they think that they will not be called to account?

(83:1-4)

Behold, (in the life to come) the truly virtuous will indeed be in bliss; on thrones they will look up (to God). You will recognise in their faces the beaming brightness of bliss.

(83:22-24)

O humans! Truly, you are ever toiling on towards your Lord—painfully toiling; but you will meet Him.

(84:6)

Those who are given their record in the right hand, soon will their account be taken by an easy reckoning, and they will turn to their people, rejoicing. But those who are given their record behind their back—soon will they cry out, lost, and will enter a blazing fire. Truly, that one went about among his people rejoicing; truly he did not think that he would have to return (to Us). No, no—his Lord was ever watchful for him.

(84:7-15)

Those who persecute the believers, men or women, and do not turn in repentance, will have the penalty of Hell; they will have the penalty of the burning fire.

(85:10)

The grip of your Lord is truly powerful. It is He Who creates from the very beginning, and can restore life. And he is the Oft-Forgiving, full of loving-kindness, Lord of the Throne of Glory, the One Who does all that His intent.

(85:12-16)

There is no soul but has a protector over it.

(86:4)

We shall make it easy for you to follow the straightforward (Path).

(87:8)

The warning will be received by those who reverence God; but it will be avoided by those most unfortunate ones, who will enter the Great Fire, in which they will then neither die nor live.

(87:10-13)

Those who purify themselves will prosper, and those who glorify the name of their Guardian-Lord, and (lift their hearts) in prayer.

(87:14-15)

Nay, but (how will you fare on Judgement Day,) when the earth is pounded to powder, and your Lord is revealed, and His angels—rank upon rank? And on that Day, Hell will be brought (within sight); on that Day people will remember. But how will that remembrance profit them then? (Those people) will say: 'Ah, would that I had provided beforehand for my life (in the Hereafter)!

(89:21-24)

(To the righteous soul will be said): 'O you, who have attained to inner peace, come back to your Lord, well pleased and well-pleasing (to Him). Enter, among those devoted to Me; Yes, enter My heaven!

(89:27-30)

The one who gives in charity and reverences God, and testifies to the Best We will indeed make smooth for him (or her) the path to Bliss.

(92:5-7)

The one who is greedy and miserly, and thinks he (or she) is self-sufficient, and calls the ultimate good a lie—We will indeed make smooth for that one the path to misery; and what will their wealth profit

them when they fall headlong? Truly it is for Us to grace (you) with guidance, and truly, Ours is (the dominion over) the life to come as well as this earlier part.

(92:8-13)

Those who spend their wealth so that they might grow in purity, and have in their minds no (thought of) payment for favours received, but only out of the longing for the Countenance of their Lord Most High; soon will they attain (complete) satisfaction.

(92:18-21)

By the glorious morning light, and by the night when it is still—your Guardian-Lord has never forsaken you, and He is not angry. And truly the Hereafter will be better for you than this present life. And soon will your Guardian-Lord give you that wherewith you will be well-pleased.

(93:1-5)

Truly, with every difficulty, there is relief.

(94:6)

When the earth is shaken with her (last) convulsion, and the earth throws up her burdens, and humanity cries (distressed) 'What is the matter with her?'–on that Day will she declare her tidings as your Lord will have inspired her to do. On that Day people come forward as separate entities, to be shown the deeds that they have done. Then shall anyone who has done an atom's weight of good, see it. And anyone who has done an atom's weight of evil shall see it.

(99:1-8)

Woe to every scandal-monger and backbiter, who piles up wealth and lays it by, thinking that this wealth would make him (or her) live for ever! By no means! They will be sure to be thrown into that which breaks to pieces.

(104:1-4)

Do you see the one who denies the judgement (to come)? Such is the person who repulses the orphan and does not encourage the feeding of the helpless poor. So woe to the worshippers who are neglectful of their prayers, those who want to be seen by others, but who refuse (to supply) the needs of their neighbours!

(107:1-7)

To you We have granted the fountain (of abundance); therefore turn to your Lord in prayer and sacrifice. For the one who hates you will be cut off.

(108:1-3)

O believers! Reverence God, and believe in His Messenger, and He will bestow upon you a double portion of His mercy; He will provide for you a light by which you shall walk, and He will forgive you; for God is Oft-Forgiving, Most Merciful.

(57:28)

So persevere patiently; for God's promise is certain; ask forgiveness for your fault, and celebrate the praises of God in the evening and in the morning.

(40:55)

Printed in India